EDON'S BOOK OF POETRY

NEVER LOSE SIGHT OF HOPE FOR IN HOPE...
YOUR DREAMS WILL COME TRUE

VJ PUBLISHING HOUSE LLC.
20461 NW 2nd Avenue   Suite 112
Miami Gardens, Florida. 33169
www.vjvjpublishinghouse.com

ISBN: 978-1-939236-14-2

LIBRARY OF CONGRESS CONTROL NUMBER:

COPYRIGHT:11/5/2021

COVER DESIGN: LUIS HIRAM ALVARADO

PRINTED IN THE UNITED STATE OF AMERICA

THIS BOOK IS PRINTED ON ACID-FREE PAPER

EDON'S BOOK OF POETRY

ACKNOWLEDGEMENTS

FIRST & FOREMOST, I GIVE THANKS TO MY Lord & Savior, Jesus Christ, and The Holy Ghost, which leads and guides me.

To my late parents, Juan R. and Concepcion Alvarado, who instilled in me Love and Respect. I still feel the Love for my late brother and sister, Jose J and Iris D. Alvarado.

To my remaining siblings Julia, Vanessa, and Carlos, we are evidence that Love truly conquers all. My sons, Luis M, Jose J., Isaac J., and only daughter Lily J. Alvarado, and my grandchildren, you are Love. To all my family & friends, thank you.

My precious wife, Denise G. Brown-Alvarado, whom I appreciate dearly, you are my heart-beat darling. To my friend and classmate, Valerie (Golden) Allen, who has been instrumental in guiding me to where I am now and articulating what God has given me throughout the years to publish, finally, you are indeed an instrument of God.

To the staff of countless workers that helped to make this possible, Bless You All!

To all the Workers in The Vineyard that I've come to know in my 37 years of Ministry, I love you all and thank you for pouring into me your wisdom, insights, pains, and victories! Glory Hallelujah!!!

Author's Bio

Luis H. Alvarado was born in Miami, Florida, in 1958 is the third child and second son of Juan R. and Concepcion, who moved to Miami, Florida, from Puerto Rico. Luis attended school in Miami and graduated from Miami Central Sr. High School where he performed in Marching and Symphonic Band and was appointed Band Captain in 1976, his Senior year.

Two years after graduating high school, Luis enlisted in The United States Army, where he served from 1978-1998, "retiring Honorably." He accepted Jesus Christ as his Lord and Savior during his service in 1979 in Schwabach, Germany. Luis began his writings while stationed at Fort Riley, Kansas. Often, he would get an urge to pick up pen and paper and start to write until the desire became words and, eventually, poetry.

Luis enjoys people and wants to share some of his life's journey with as many as possible. His journey hasn't been all peaches and cream. Like everyone else, his response always made a difference; however, Luis chose to put it on paper.

Introduction

Edon's book of poetry is a combination of poems inspired mainly by The Holy Spirit of God. Some verses are spiritually encouraging and enlightening, while others show the romantic side of the Author. There are also some tragic events that he experienced along his journey. However, because of God's Grace, he's still here to share his valley and mountaintop experiences. Our prayer is that this book finds you encouraged, inspired, refreshed, and gives you a few laughs.

Blessings always to all...

Through It All...

Life hasn't always been Good to me
And yet
I'm still standing
As you can see
Storms have come
And gone
But I've never
Had to face
Any alone
For in my storms
God gave me peace
And in due time
Those storms
Dark and dreary clouds
Ceased...
But God
Always remained near
To see me through
To the other side
And in His perfect will
I must abide
He cares for me
More than I would know
And to this dying world
He will show
His love to all
Who will receive
For He will supply

All our needs
God waits for you
To give Him a call
And He will take you
Like me
Through it all...

More Than Friends

Her lips are tender
Yet so sweet
Longing for ours
To meet
Yearning for her
In my arms so tight
Knowing what I feel inside
Is so right!
Feeling her warmth
Right next to me
Anticipation
Of what will be
As we bare our bodies
To each other
Knowing that we
Belong together
Rhythmic motion
Through-out the night
Feeling a passion
That feels so right
An eruption
Deep in my soul
Realizing that she's
The one
Who makes me whole
Our passions
Burn with utter desire
Taking each other
Higher and Higher!

Till at last
We both reach the end
Knowing that we are
More than friends…

"As It Rains"

Wanting you here
For us to share
Wanting to show you
How much I really care
In you I've found
A diamond in the rough
Caring, Compassionate
And all that good stuff
If you and I
Were ever able to be
There is so much
We could share till eternity
Watching the rain
Fall from God's blue sky
Thinking to myself
Of so many reasons why
You come to my mind
On this rainy day
Realizing
That you're seven digits away
Watching the water flow
Whence it drains
All of this crossed my mind
As it rains…

Can It Be?

Can it be
That I'm here still alive?
Waiting and working
Until my Savoir arrives
Trying to do what is best
For me to do
Praying for others
And also praying for you
Here I am
On a solid rock to stay
Now that my feet
Are out of the mirky clay
Come and see
What we all have to do
Can it be?
Yes!
My Savior is also calling you...

Be Still And Know That I Am

We all seem to be in a hurry to
nowhere fast
We don't know
if what we have will last
Because others are willing
to give me a try
You can also call
I'm standing by
Whatever your cares are
Give them all to Me
Trust Me and love Me
and you will see
Just how much
I really care for you
You'll find out that no
other love will do
My love is pure and
most of all
I'm waiting for you to
give Me that call
I'll answer you
Morning, noon, and night
All of your dark times
I'll make them bright
I gave My Son
To rid the world of sin
He is the doorway
for you to come in
And reign with Me

through-out eternity
I long to have you
right here with Me
You're more than
just a face or a name
to me
You're the reason
I was hung on that tree
Blessed you are
and will always be
Be Still and Know That I am...

You Are

A face in the crowd
A voice from afar
Some may wonder
Just who you are
They only know
Just what they see
Only God knows
Who you are to be
Going thru life
With the joys and pains
Just when you see the sun
It begins to rain
Clouds may cover
And darken your skies
But he watches over you
With His eyes
Knowing your weakness
And your strength
You go far
But you're at His arm's length
Standing and waiting
For you to call
Because it's you
He loves most of all
When life's not what you
Want it to be
Just call His name
And you will see
He'll turn your dark days
To marvelous light

Lean and depend on him
It's not your fight
The victory you have
Has already been won
Because of Calvary
And God's only Son
When at night you see
That twinkling star
Just "Remember"
He made you
Who you are...

You're The One

You're the one who
I can lean on
When this world seems to
Leave me feeling alone
You're the one
Who makes me smile
You make all my hard times
Worth the while
You're the one
Who watches over me
Keeping me from drowning
In the raging sea
Of all the cares
Of this life
Yes, you're the one
Who paid the price
You're the one
Who has redeemed us
Yes, you're my Friend
And your name is
Jesus...

Heaven

I've never been there
But I'd like to go
To see the things
I've read about
Things I just don't know
The streets are paved
With gold I've been told
A place where nothing
Never gets old
A city as new
Like a newborn baby
Where there is no such thing
As a man or a lady
A place where
We're all and one the same
Praising and singing
In Jesus's mighty name!!!

Patience (A Poem Of Job)

Time goes by
And we seem to stand still
We wonder how
We'll get over that hill
Around us many
Are moving really fast
But what they have
Just won't last
Zealous, I may be
But I cannot go
Until God shows
And lets me know
When the time has come
For me to journey on
Because I'm free
There was a man
Who had to wait
Yes, he'll be there
At the Pearly gate
Everything he had
Was taken away
But he trusted in God
Day by day
Even his friends
Talked about him really bad
But he knew that the Lord
Was all he had
They wouldn't give up
And leave him alone
But he knew about the love

That God had shown
In God's hands
He placed his body and soul
By and by God raised
And made him whole
What did cause him
To humble himself
And wait
Knowing that God
Would never be late
Who gave him back
All that he had lost
What is this, you might ask?
IT'S PATIENCE!

Understanding

Lord, I realize that
In due time
I'll know all the things
That you have to show
To my soul in this old
World of sin
Things that hurt
Very deep within
Loves ones come
And love ones go
No matter which way
This I know
That you hold the answers
In your hand
Answers to the trials
Of this land
Sometimes we feel hurt
And we feel pain
Just like the sun shines
There must be rain
Snow comes and covers
The pretty green grass
And all seems lost
Until at last…
The sun comes out
And melts the snow away
And gives the earth life
And a brand-new day
Resurrection from what
Once seemed to be death

God gives us that
Ever-lasting breath
That lives on forever
And ever more
Knowing God has much
More in store
For them who heed
And obey
And listen to what
The Spirit has to say
Lord, I don't wish
To sound anyways demanding
I just ask for a little more
Understanding…

Who Knows?

It is said
That tomorrow
Is just another day
But what will
It bring?
Who am I to say?
It is said
that tomorrow
Will never get here
But don't you Worry
And don't you fear
When it comes
It will be today
And in time
Tomorrow will Become yesterday
Who named the day
Just as they are?
For tomorrow and yesterday
Always seem so far
Tomorrow
For some
Will be too far to reach
As for yesterday
We grasp the lessons
Each day teach
As they come
They will also go
Like the rivers
We see how
They flow

Wonder how the day comes
And how it goes
Where do they end
Who knows?

I Ain't Going Nowhere

Your love captivated me
Right from the start
It was true and pure
So, I gave you my heart
Thinking about you
Each and every day
Knowing that I would always
Have words to say
How I felt deep within my soul
You are the one
Who makes my life whole
Giving up myself to be
There for you
Knowing that what I feel
Is love that's true
Sharing my inner thoughts
With you each day
Before I slept
Each night I would pray
For our love to mature
And grow strong
Because it's you that
My heart longs
And that God keep you
In His loving care
Mislead or deceive you
I wouldn't dare
The joy and laughter
You bring to my heart
Knowing that one day

I would be that part
That completes this puzzle
That we call life
By being your husband
And you my wife
And just so you know
I really do care
I can honestly say
'I ain't going nowhere'

Get Ready For The Overflow

You can't beat
God's giving
This I know is true
For all that you give
Will find its way back to you
Doesn't matter what you give
Money, time, words or love
Rest assured blessings
Will shower down from above
The more you give
The more
He will give back
Concerning your giving
Never count God as slack
He's always there to provide
All your needs
He sometimes blesses us
Even when we fail to heed
To His word to bring our offerings
And tithes nevertheless,
To us He will always provide
His love that is true
And so divine
His love within us
Will break through
And shine
For this world to behold And also see
He died for you
Just like He died for me
His giving to behold

Is such a marvelous site
When God gives back
He does it right!
So, when your cup seems
To be empty or low
Fret not, it's just room
That's made for the overflow

Inspired by: Verlene Dickson
A true friend who is loved by
God...

Smiles

They come so few
And in between
But when it does
It can be seen
Some can set
The heart aglow
Showing your happiness
For the world to know
Some radiate like
The Sun that shines
Telling the world that
'I feel fine'
Some can turn
Your darkness into light
When they come shining
through so very bright
In time of need
They come to us
To help us resolve
Difficulties without a fuss
When shining bright
It can be seen for miles
Yeah, I'm talking about your smiles...

HERE AM I

The world is full of
God's Great Glory
Many a men
Have disputed
His story
One day
He will reveal
Himself to all
If we're not ready
On whose name
Can we call?
He comes quickly
With rewards
In His loving Hands
To give to every humble
And obedient man
When He comes
And cracks the sky
I'll say Lord have mercy!
Here am I...

Pressing

I write these few lines
On pressing
I want you to understand
What I'm stressing
For you see you will get
A beautiful blessing
If you hold on
And keep on pressing
God only knows how much
We can take
Sometimes we may bend
But God will never allow us to break
You see Jesus died
For our lost sake
When He comes back
With Him
He will take
Those who went through
And held on to His name
Those who through all their
Trials
His name wasn't put to shame
God is merciful both
Now and forever
He said He won't leave you
No, no never!
As I write
These very few lines
God says to me
'You're still mine

Jesus, Jesus!
My only true and faithful friend
You will always be with me
until the very end
I'm so grateful
that you're so good
I'm trying to live the life that I should
If sometimes I fall
Short of your Glory
Then Lord I'll just say
'Please remember me'

You

Some would say it's not
worth the while
But I say that the world is
beautiful when you smile
When others are not really what
they seem to be
Then I'll open my arms
for you to come unto Me
Lay your head on My shoulder
and I'll give you rest
When you think about it
I care for you the best
Even when you're lonely just
look to the sky
Call My name and you'll see
Me standing by
I'm waiting for you to walk
and talk with Me
I can fix all of your problems just try
Me and see
I gave My life
so, you could live without fear
Freely I gave it, and now I'm
always near
Near to heed
and answer your call
Because it's you
that I watch over
most of all
So, when this world keeps

letting you down
Just call My name,
I'll be around
I'm your friend
Brother, Sister
Mother and Father
and all that you need
I just ask that you would
only heed
To My words
and obey
My voice
It's up to you,
It's your choice.......

Being With You

Something…
That I always look forward to
No matter what the day
Has for me to do
As busy as I get
I want it that much more
Bringing joy to my heart
Right down to the core
Patiently waiting for that
Time to finally come
Sometimes singing
Other times just a hum
Melodies that touches me
Deep in my heart
Wondering how long
Must we be apart
In due time
it Will all come to be
In my mind visions
Of what I see
Every day it reappears again
So, brand new
The very thought of just
Being with you

The Thought Of You

Early in the Morning
And it's no surprise
There, present
The moment
I open my eyes
After I shower
It's still there
Even after I'm done
Combing my hair
Following me
As I sit down to eat
It goes with me
As I leave my seat
Out the door
And here it still come
At times it feels brighter
Then the morning sun
Start my day
At the beginning of the week
Always present
I never have to seek
Never hidden
Always in plain view
Always with me
It's the thought of you...

AT CALVARY

Since the beginning of time
man doesn't understand
The truth about the master's
plan man has tried
everything to refute it
But in the end
no one can dispute it
Every imagination conceived
in attempt to disclaim
What God in His word has
given us to proclaim
Truth be told man will never
give up trying
To make us believe that the
Bible is lying
About how much
God really loves us
And by the shedding of His blood
He has redeemed us all
that's been done or said
contrary to the story
God in the end will
receive His glory
Every knee shall bow
every tongue confess
To those who believe
We are already blessed
God gave His Son
that the world might live
Ask for His mercy

and He will forgive
Be washed and cleaned
whiter than snow
You are of the redeemed
let the world know
We belong to God
can't you all see
Yes, it was all finished
at CALVARY...

A Prepared Table

In this life
we have our ups and downs
Knowing that trouble is
always hanging around
Yet we endure
the hardships and the pain
Along with the sunshine
there, cometh rain
But the rain in time
helps us to grow
What others see
they will know
Through it all
we have overcome
All of the heartaches
and then some
More than we can
ever think to say
The doors will open
and we will find our way
Knowing that our God
is always able To lead us
To…
His prepared table

Chances Are

Chances are…
that you
will read this
Chances are…
that you won't
Chances that…
I will write
another one
Chances are…
that I don't
Some Chances…
are good
some are not
We don't know
what our
Chances are…
If we don't take one
What are your
Chances?

And He Knows

Some trials come slow
and some real fast
But we realize that
they won't last
At times they come and
catch us unaware
But we must always be mindful
of all the snares
That we don't get
lured into the trap
By using God's word
we have our own map
To help us navigate
along our way
Yes, His word
will guide us day by day
To make it into His kingdom
where we will find rest
When we're at our worst
He's at His best
He will always be there
to see us through
No matter what
that old devil tries
to do
Keeping the faith
and never letting go
In due time to us
He will show
That He will never

leave us never
No, no!
Trials may come
and trials may go
God sees it all
and he knows...

In God's Hand

I knew someone who
became my friend
But his life would come to a
very tragic end
We were co-workers
at one point of time
But that all changed
with the times
He ventured out
to live in the streets
Never knowing
that out there he would meet
Evil and darkness
from day to day
Whenever I saw him
I just had to say
My friend it's time
to get back on your feet
He looks at me
as though that thing call defeat
Had taken over his spirit and his soul
His eyes became dark
and very cold
As he lay asleep
that dreadful night
Evil approached
and snuffed out his life
Why would anyone want
to hurt a lonely man?
I don't know

but I pray he's in God's hand....

Ode to my friend Todd Hill
Murdered December 22, 2008 on the streets of Miami, Florida

What About Us (United States Veterans)?

They have answered the call, in vast amounts
So many have sacrificed, too many to count
They are truly, a very special breed
Sent out to bid, our leader's deeds
To the front lines, many will go
How many will return, nobody will know
They proceed to give, that ultimate sacrifice
Trying so hard, not to lose their life
Sent far away, to protect us all
Armed and prepared, to answer the call
Yet when they return, all seems so lost
Giving their all, but at what cost?
Some lose limbs, minds, even their lives
To those who do return, it's a world full of strife
Needing help, just to make it through
I hope and pray that, this doesn't happen to you
Many have fallen, between the cracks
No-one to care, when they return back
It's a crying shame, the way we treat our Vets
Society has taken better care, of their own pets
A better healthcare, is what they need now
They can't find it, nowhere, no how
Trying to navigate
The bureaucratic red tape
Then for some, it will be far too late
Millions of dollars, have already been given
For a better life, for them to be living
Yet far too many, still are living in the streets
Searching and begging, for a bite to eat
We treat them just, like yesterday's trash

Keeping our pockets, filled with ill-gotten cash
Try putting yourself, in their place
Experience the reality, of society's face
When it thumbs, its nose up to you
Yes, these are the things, our Veterans go through
And yet you still wonder, what's all the fuss
They, just want the questioned answered
What about us?

Like He Said He Would

There are times
When just can't see our way
Seems like the storms of life Get worse day by day
Every now and then
A little Sunshine breaks through
And then again the clouds
Darken our skies anew
Thunder clasps roar
Through our lives
And we despair
Not realizing
That there is someone
Who really truly cares
The rain in our lives
Washes our dreams
Down the drain
Leaving us to wonder
If things will be the same
Testing our faith
With the winds that blow
What's coming next
Well, we don't really know
Day breaks
And the sun comes
Shining through
Leaving us with His promise
He will take care of you
Giving us a new lease on life
And feeling really good
God always keeps His promises
Just like 'He said He would

Strength

Strength comes from
Heaven above
From God Almighty
Through His love
His love that went to
Calvary
His love that died
To set us free
His love rose again
On the third day
His love is now
Shining the way
To His Kingdom
Of which we strive
For a Kingdom of Heavenly
Things that He has in store
For us to receive
As freely as we may
Till He parts the clouds
One unknown day
He gives us strength
to hold onto His hand
For someday
We will reach the Promised Land
His strength for us
Is all in one
This strength I speak of is
His only begotten Son
God's blessings comes
in all shapes and sizes

God's blessings are so full
of so many surprises!
That brings bundles of joy
to our heart
Joy that cannot keep
His true Saints apart
Jesus is love
Jesus is love...

Shelter In The Time Of Storm

In our lives
We have ups and down
We face them all
With either a smile or a frown
Many are the obstacles
That we must overcome
What may seem easy to some
Maybe hard for one
Yet we cannot surrender
To the trials of this life
Even when we encounter hatred
Envy and strife
From day one
Our lives are filled with trouble
But I know someone
Who will be there on the double
When it seems
Like no one else can understand
My God is very able
And I believe He can
Guide us through
Each and every day
Especially when we can't
Find our way
When others seem to be
Uncaring and cold
He will answer us
If we would be so bold
To call Him up
In our time of need

He's always there to provide
A good deed
Even in the cold
He will keep us warm
He is our
'Shelter in the time of a Storm'

The Dreamer

The place seems
Familiar yet so strange
The thoughts of my mind
Had to be arranged
I've been here before
But how can that be
For all around me
Is not what I really see
Trees, cars, buildings
People and stores
Wait a minute
There is so much more
Yes, I know
I've been here at some time
But how could that be
It was all in my mind
It all seemed so real
Too real to be true
Yet most of all
I remember seeing you
Your beauty came
Shining all around
You spoke to me
Yet I heard no sound
I wanted to hold
And caress you in my arms
I was turned on by your beauty
And your charm
As I reached for you
You faded away

My eyes opened up
And I heard myself say
'What's going on?
Where did you go?'
Tell me please
I just have to know
Then I realized
I was just the dreamer...

My Vision

Seeing is believing
Is what they all say
Until I saw it
In another way
I saw it from the beginning
Until the end
I saw it from the outside
And from within
I saw it from the bottom
And from the top
As I kept on looking
It just wouldn't stop
I saw near
And I saw it from afar
I saw it glow
Like the Bright and Morning Star
I saw it come
And then I saw it go
I saw it become dim
And then start to glow
I saw that it was truly
One of a kind
What I saw
It stayed deep in my mind
Was it real
Or was it fake?
Then I saw it come
For me to take
Away from this world
Full of sin

It opened up its doors
Beckoning me to come in
I saw the streets
Were paved with pure gold
I saw that in it
Nothing would ever get old
A Tree Of Life
Stood in its midst
Then I wondered
What kind of world is this
As I stood there
He came to me
The one who was hung
On Calvary's tree
I've come for you
Is what He said
Then I wondered
If I was already dead
My eyes opened up
As I began to cry
I heard Him say
"I'm standing by"
Leading and guiding
You along the way
For you see, it was for you
That I died that day
From my eyes
The tears began to fall
I dropped to my knees
And began to call
To my Savior

Who loves me so
Now I want
The whole world
To know
It's time for you
To make your decision
Maybe then you too
Will see my vision...

www.ingramcontent.com/pod-product-compliance
Lightning Source LLC
LaVergne TN
LVHW041209080426
835508LV00008B/868